# GET INTO ART

# PLACES

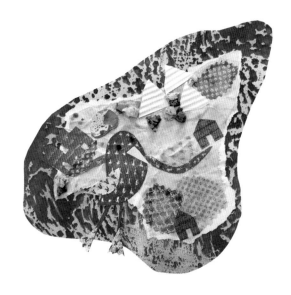

## SUSIE BROOKS

KINGFISHER

First published 2014 by Kingfisher
an imprint of Macmillan Children's Books
20 New Wharf Road, London N1 9RR
Associated companies throughout the world
www.panmacmillan.com

Edited by Catherine Brereton and Polly Goodman
Designed by Peter Clayman
Cover design by Jane Tassie
Project photography by Peter Clayman
Picture research by AME Picture Research

ISBN 978-0-7534-3740-7 (HB)
ISBN 978-0-7534-3854-1 (PB)

9 8 7 6 5 4 3 2 1
1TR/0615/LFG/UG/128MA
A CIP catalogue record for this book is available from the British Library.
Printed in China

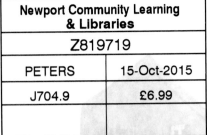

## Picture credits

The Publisher would like to thank the following for permission to reproduce their material.
Every care has been taken to trace copyright holders.
Top = t; Bottom = b; Centre = c; Left = l; Right = r
Cover and page 6 *Bedroom in Arles* by Vincent van Gogh/The Art Archive/Musée d'Orsay Paris/Collection Dagli Orti;
page 4 *Winter Landscape* by Wassily Kandinsky/The Gallery Collection/Corbis ©ADAGP, Paris and DACS, London 2014;
8 *The Grand Canal in Venice with San Simeone Piccolo* by Giovanni Antonio Canaletto/The Art Archive/DeA Picture
Library/G. Nimatallah; 10 *Landscape in Ceret* by Juan Gris/The Art Archive/Moderna Museet Stockholm/Gianni Dagli
Orti; 12 *Castle and Sun* by Paul Klee/The Gallery Collection/Corbis; 14 *Fuji in Clear Weather* by Katsushika Hokusai/The
Art Archive/British Museum/Superstock; 16 *Sainte Adresse by Night* by Raoul Dufy/The Art Archive/Musée des Beaux
Arts Nancy/Gianni Dagli Orti t ©ADAGP, Paris and DACS, London 2014; 18 Aboriginal painting/The Art Archive/DeA
Picture Library; 20 *Winter Landscape* by Wassily Kandinsky/The Gallery Collection/Corbis ©ADAGP, Paris and DACS,
London 2014; 22 *Coming Out of School* by L. S. Lowry/The Art Archive/Tate Gallery London/Superstock ©The Estate of
L.S. Lowry. All Rights Reserved, DACS 2014; 24 *Iceland Showing Volcano Hecla* by Abraham Ortelius/The Art Archive/
Bodleian Library Oxford, Arch Bb9 plate 98; 26 *New York Under Gaslight* by Stuart Davis/The Israel Museum, Jerusalem,
Israel/Gift of Rebecca Shulman, New York/The Bridgeman Art Library ©Estate of Stuart Davis/DACS, London/VAGA,
New York 2014; 28 *The Human Condition* by Rene Magritte/The Art Archive/Private Collection/Gianni Dagli Orti
©ADAGP, Paris and DACS, London 2014. Paint splodge motif throughout Shutterstock/RLN.

# CONTENTS

# PICTURE A PLACE

**Do you have a favourite place you'd like to put in a picture?**
Maybe it's your room, a park, a shop, or somewhere you've been
on holiday! The world is full of exciting places that give artists
ideas for their work. Country landscapes, buzzing cities, beaches,
bedrooms, racetracks – even outer space – can be subjects for art.
And you don't have to go anywhere to dream up imaginary places!

**See how places have inspired famous artists –**
then **let them inspire you too!** Each page of this book
will tell you about a work of art and the person who
created it. When you lift the flap, you'll find a project
based on the artwork. Don't feel you have to copy it
exactly. Half the fun of art is exploring your own ideas!

## GETTING STARTED

There's a checklist on page 31 that will tell you
what you need for each project, but it's a good idea
to read through the steps before you begin. There
are also some handy tips on the next page...

Always have a **pencil** and
**rubber** handy. Making a
rough **sketch** can help you
plan a project and see how
it's going to look.

# PICK YOUR PAINT...

**Acrylic paints** are thick and bright – they're great for strong colours, or textures like grass.

**Ready-mix paints** are cheaper than acrylics but still bright. Use them when you need lots of paint.

**Watercolours** give a thinner colouring that you can build up in layers, called washes.

Use a mixture of thick and thin **paintbrushes**. Have a jam jar or plastic cup of water ready to rinse them in and a **palette** or paper plate for mixing paint.

acrylic paint

Lay some newspaper on your surface before you start to paint!

watercolour paint

# TRY PASTELS...

**Oil pastels** have a bright, waxy look, like crayons. **Soft pastels** can be smudged and blended like chalk.

sponged paint

For painting, use thick **cartridge** or **watercolour paper** – anything too thin will wrinkle. **Pastel paper** has a rough surface that holds onto the colour.

Collect a range of **coloured papers and card** for collage and 3-D models.

oil pastels

soft pastels

Ready to start?
Let's **get into art!**

**Look around at home for other art materials.** Useful things include sponges, rags or cloths, scissors, glue, cling film, cocktail sticks, drinking straws and bubble wrap.

# BRUSH A BEDROOM

## Paint your own bedroom **in chunky brushstrokes like Van Gogh!**

**1** On a piece of thick paper, draw the outline of your room. Don't worry about getting it exactly right – if it's a bit higgledy-piggledy it will be more like Van Gogh's!

*Tidy up first so you don't have to paint too many fiddly bits!*

**2** On a paper plate, mix acrylic paint with some PVA glue to thicken it. Paint the larger areas first, laying the colour on thickly with a wide brush.

*Don't try to go right to the edges – you can fill in the gaps at the end.*

**3** While the paint is still wet, scrape patterns into it with a cocktail stick, fork, or the end of your brush.

*You can swirl two colours together if you like!*

**4** Carry on painting and scraping different textures. Finally, fill in any gaps using a fine brush.

*If you want to add extra details, wait for the paint to dry first.*

# BEDROOM IN ARLES

Vincent van Gogh 1889

**If you made a list of places where you spend a lot of time, your bedroom would probably be one of them.** Van Gogh decided to paint a picture of his – three times!

## Restful room

Van Gogh's room is very tidy! He wanted us to feel restful when we look at it. There's a big comfy bed and sunlight streaming through the window; the colours are warm and bright. We see the artist's smocks hanging up, and the blue jug and bowl he used for washing. It's a calm, simple scene… but can you spot anything unusual?

Look at the doors – they're both blocked by furniture. The pictures make the wall seem to lean in, and the floor slopes down towards us. Van Gogh has used thick, chunky brushstrokes and bold outlines instead of shadows. All these things stop the scene from being too ordinary!

## WHO WAS VAN GOGH?

Vincent van Gogh was born in the Netherlands in 1853. He began painting in his famous colourful style after a move to France in the 1880s, but he struggled to sell his work. Poor and mentally ill, Vincent ended his life aged 37. In 10 years he had made an impressive 900 paintings! They sell for millions today.

# Follow these steps to draw a row of houses and trees

## IN PERSPECTIVE

**1** With a ruler and pencil, draw a line straight across the page. This is the horizon (h). Mark a point along the line. This is the vanishing point (v). Draw diagonal lines from the vanishing point to the edges of the page, as shown.

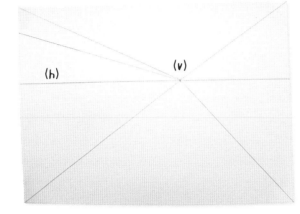

**2** For the houses, draw the vertical lines (a) first. Follow the diagonal lines to draw walls going away from you (b). For the side walls, draw lines straight across (c).

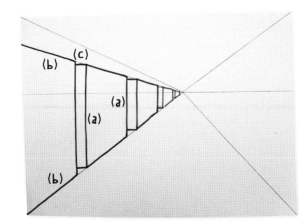

**3** Use the top diagonal line to draw the roofs. You can add chimneys if you like. On the opposite side of the page, draw a row of trees between the diagonal lines.

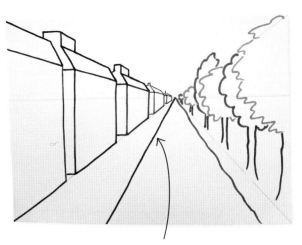

Draw lines for the road and verge, both meeting at the vanishing point.

**4** Draw in the detail. Use a ruler to help make sure all lines going away from you lead to the vanishing point.

Cut out a figure and place it on the page. What happens if you move it into the distance?

# GRAND CANAL
## WITH SAN SIMEONE PICCOLO

Canaletto, *about* 1740

**Imagine rowing a boat into the distance of this scene – it looks like a long way!**
Of course it's just a flat painting, but Canaletto has managed to create an amazing sense of space.

## A place to remember

Do you recognize this place? It's Venice, the famous Italian city. In the days before photography, tourists liked to take home paintings or drawings to remind them of their stay there. Canaletto was popular for his many detailed views, or *vedute*, of the city.

In this wide-angle picture, our eye travels from the busy foreground boats, past beautiful buildings, all the way to the distant canal bend. Canaletto draws us in using his skill at perspective, where things look smaller as they get further away. He was brilliant at capturing light and reflections on the water. One person said he could make the sun shine in his work!

### WHO WAS CANALETTO?

Giovanni Antonio Canal was born in Venice in 1697. He was nicknamed Canaletto ('little Canal') because his father was an artist too. Both men worked as theatre scenery painters, but Canaletto later switched to painting large canvases showing daily life in Venice and England.

# SLICE A SCENE

## Mix and match night and day **in this Cubist chop-up painting!**

**1** Draw a line down the middle of a piece of thick white paper. One side will be night; the other day. Sketch a landscape across the page, using simple lines and shapes.

Make some house and tree shapes big and close-up, and others small and distant.

**2** Now you can paint the scene. Do a bright sky and sunny colours on one side, and a dark sky and dimmer colours on the other.

You don't have to be too neat – let your brushstrokes show!

**3** When your finished painting is dry, cut it into strips. Make some wider than others – it doesn't matter if your cutting goes a bit wonky.

**4** Jumble up your painted strips to create a new scene. Turn some of them upside-down. Glue them onto a piece of coloured paper, leaving a border like a frame around the edge.

Overlap some strips if you need to, or leave narrow gaps between a few of them!

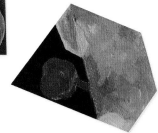

If you compare this picture to the one on page 8, you'll see it looks much flatter. Gris and the Cubists thought that painting in perspective was far too limited! They wanted to show the world from many angles, not just a single viewpoint. This break from tradition shocked people at the time.

# LANDSCAPE AT CERET

Juan Gris 1913

**No one has cut up this picture, but it looks a bit like a jigsaw puzzle!** Gris wanted to show a landscape in lots of ways at once, so he painted it in patchwork pieces.

## Kaleidoscope world

Look at the buildings in the middle. There are tiled rooftops seen from above, walls from the side and some even upside-down! The trees and hills are juggled around, so we see them from different viewpoints. It seems to be daytime with the bright, sunny colours – but there are hints of night darkness too. It's like a kaleidoscope of memories of a place!

Gris and other artists who painted in this style were known as Cubists. They loved to play around with space and shapes. They took parts of what they saw or remembered, and rearranged them in exciting ways.

## WHO WAS GRIS?

Juan Gris was born in Spain in 1887, but spent most of his working life in France. He was inspired by the leading Cubists, Pablo Picasso and Georges Braque. The world around them was changing, and photography was starting to replace realistic art. Cubism became a modern way of painting!

# CASTLE AND MOON

## Choose night-time colours **for this moonlit castle mosaic!**

**1** You'll need two large sheets of paper – one light-coloured and the other dark. On the light paper, sketch the outline of a castle and moon.

*Keep the drawing simple – it's just a guide!*

**2** Cut out your mosaic pieces from different coloured papers. Starting in one corner, arrange them like a puzzle to fill in the castle. Glue them down.

*Leave a small gap between the pieces, so they look like tiles.*

**3** When your castle is complete, cut it out. Leave a narrow border of the light-coloured paper around the edge.

**4** Stick your castle onto the dark sheet of paper. Cut out a bright moon and glue it on.

*You could add a couple more mosaic blocks at the sides.*

# CASTLE AND SUN

Paul Klee 1928

**This castle doesn't look as if it would stand for thousands of years – but it makes an impressive picture!** Klee has built it up from lots of multicoloured blocks, like a mosaic.

### Rainbow walls

Klee was clever with colour. The way he arranged the blocks makes us feel we're looking at a castle, even though there's no real outline. We can pick out bright battlements, turrets, an archway and the sun, which zing out against darker areas. The design makes our eyes dart around the page!

Klee loved playing with geometric shapes to create magical designs and patterns. He often worked on several very different canvases at once. This painting is almost abstract, because you can't immediately tell what it is. The warm, cheery colours and jostling shapes seem to take on a life of their own!

## WHO WAS KLEE?

Paul Klee was born in Switzerland in 1879. As a boy he was good at music, but he soon discovered a talent for drawing, too. After a trip to Tunisia he fell in love with colour, which became the main focus of his painting. By the time he died in 1940, he had more than 9,000 works to his name!

# MOUNT SPLATTER

## You can recreate this erupting volcano **as many times as you like!**

**1** To make a printing plate, cut out a volcano and smoke shapes from a spongy kitchen cloth. Stick them with craft glue onto cardboard – the back of an old sketchbook is good.

Add some shapes for land or water in the foreground.

**2** When the glue is dry, cover the shapes thickly with acrylic paint. You can swirl two colours together for a streaky effect. While the paint is still wet, press it down firmly onto red paper.

When you peel off the printing plate, the print underneath will be in reverse!

**4** Wipe off any excess paint from the printing plate and let it dry a bit. Then try printing and splattering with some different colours!

**3** Let the paint dry before you erupt your volcano! Water down some red and yellow paint and drop a little onto the summit. Blow through a straw to make it trickle down the sides.

Lay down plenty of newspaper for this bit!

Finish by splattering paint over the page with the flick of a brush.

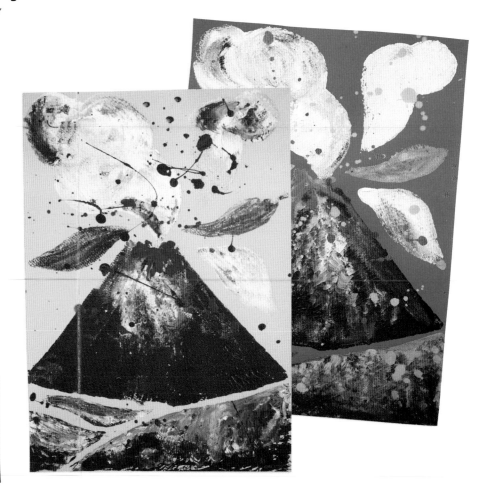

# MOUNT FUJI
## IN CLEAR WEATHER

Katsushika Hokusai, about 1831

**Could you draw the same place again and again?** Hokusai so loved Mount Fuji, he designed more than 140 different prints of it! This one comes from a series of 36 views.

## Varied views

Hokusai's prints show Mount Fuji from the north, south, east, west… close up and far away. In this one, the snow-drizzled cone of the volcano glows red under a scattering of clouds. Notice how the trees look like specks on its giant slopes. The sky is printed in Prussian blue – a colour that was new to Japan at the time. It helped to make *36 Views of Mount Fuji* a smash hit!

Hokusai used a printing technique called *ukiyo-e*. He would make a drawing, then an assistant would glue it face down on a block of wood and cut away the blank areas. The block was inked and pressed onto paper, then more blocks were made to print each colour of the scene.

### WHO WAS HOKUSAI?

**Katsushika Hokusai was born in 1760 in Japan. He wasn't called Hokusai then – he changed his name many times throughout his life! Fascinated by drawing from the age of six, he enjoyed a long career as an artist. When he made his famous Mount Fuji prints, he was about 70 years old!**

# SUNSET STRIPS

## Doodle like Dufy **on a tissue paper background!**

**1** First sketch out your scene on a piece of thick white paper. Draw a line for the horizon, a sun, some boats, umbrellas and people. Try to suggest the shapes in just a few lines!

Press quite hard so you can see the lines through tissue paper.

**2** Now tear some strips of tissue paper. Glue them down, one at a time, to make a fiery sky. Stick a round, red sun on top, then start on the sea.

You can layer light strips over dark to make different colours.

**4** When the background is dry, go over your pencil lines with an oil pastel or soft wax crayon. Doodle quickly – you don't have to be too accurate!

**3** To make sunny reflections, stick small pieces of orange, pink and yellow tissue paper over the sea.

You could add some wiggly lines for waves.

# NIGHT AT SAINTE ADRESSE

Raoul Dufy, late 1920s–1930s

**Do you love the seaside?**
**We can tell Raoul Dufy did!**
His painting conjures up a calm, contented feeling as the sun goes down over a rippling ocean.

**Sketchy scene**
Look at the people strolling along here – they are sketched in just a few lines. Dufy didn't worry about details like faces! We can see there are umbrellas, and boats in the distance, but they're suggested by very simple marks. Instead of painting a realistic view, Dufy gives us an impression of the place.

Dufy's brushstrokes are thick and almost scribbly. They make everything seem to move. Bright reflections dance across the water and a warm, peachy glow fills the sky. Unlike traditional artists, who faded things into the distance to create a sense of space, Dufy painted vibrant colours all over his canvases!

## WHO WAS DUFY?

Raoul Dufy was born in France in 1877. He grew up by the seaside, along with his eight brothers and sisters. Dufy liked to paint the joyful things in life, from beach scenes to horse races and sailing regattas. With his colourful, decorative style, he was also a successful fabric designer.

# DOTTY DESIGNS

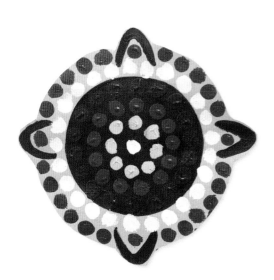

Some Australian Aboriginal paintings reveal how to find a sacred site or waterhole, like magical maps that only those who know the land can read! Others illustrate stories from the Dreamtime, when Australian Aboriginal people believe the world was created. Many paintings feature animals, their tracks, plants, food or the weather. Everything has its own symbol, which is read in a special way.

Look on the Internet for patterns and symbols used in Australian Aboriginal art, **then go dotty with this finger painting!**

**1** Sketch the main shapes of your design on a piece of orange, yellow or brown paper.

**2** Using a paintbrush and dark-coloured paint, fill in the lines and a few of the shapes.

**3** Now squeeze some paint onto a paper plate or palette. Dip your fingertip into a colour, then press it onto the page. You can print a few dots before dipping into more paint. Print one colour at a time!

To fit within a circle, you might have to space some dots more than others.

**4** Carry on dipping and dotting until you've filled the whole page!

# ABORIGINAL DOT PAINTING

Australian Aboriginal artist

**This may not look like an obvious place, but that's what the artist intended!** Australian Aboriginal dot paintings tell secret stories about the land and how the world was created.

## Ancient art

Aboriginal peoples were the first to live in Australia. Their history and art traditions go back many thousands of years. This painting is a modern one, but it illustrates an ancient story in a way that only certain people can understand.

Every shape and pattern we see here means something. The circles may be campsites, watering holes or meeting places, while the U-shapes represent people. There are snakes, honey ants and other symbols relating to the landscape and beliefs about it. Australian Aboriginal people have no written language, so paintings like this are a great way to pass information down through family lines.

## HOW WAS IT MADE?

**Traditional Australian Aboriginal art takes many forms, from painting on rocks or bark to making pictures in the desert sand. Dot painting on canvas like this began in the 1970s. The artists use acrylic paints in earthy colours, such as browns, ochres and greens. To make the dots, they dip in the end of a stick.**

# RAINBOW SNOW

## See how colours make you feel **with these no-white snow scenes!**

**1** First sketch out your scene on a piece of red or orange pastel paper. Using a yellow chalk or pastel, start to colour patches of it in.

**2** Add patches of other warm, light colours such as orange and pink. You can blend colours together using your finger, or let parts of the background show through.

Use softer, duller colours in the distance.

**3** Add darker colours for trees and shadows last.

**4** Try recreating your scene using cool colours such as pale blues and greens. See how different it feels!

Experiment with as many different colours as you like!

Very pale colours look almost white against the darker paper.

# WINTER LANDSCAPE

Wassily Kandinsky 1909

**What colour is snow?** You might say 'white', but to Kandinsky it was all the colours of the rainbow! There's hardly any white at all in this painting of a wintry scene.

## Cosy snow

Sometimes when you look at a snowy landscape, you can see hints of pink, blue and yellow as sunlight shimmers across it. Kandinsky took this idea to extremes. He 'turned up' the colours in his painting so they are extra bold and bright. He laid them down in big, chunky brushstrokes.

Colours were really important to Kandinsky. He used them to show us not how his world looked, but how he felt about it. We know that snow is cold, but his pinks, oranges and yellows warm it up like a cosy blanket! The little house glows invitingly against the cool blue shadows of a winter's day.

## WHO WAS KANDINSKY?

Wassily Kandinsky was born in Russia in 1866. From a young age, he felt affected by colours and even said they made him hear different musical sounds. Eventually, Kandinsky's paintings became more about colour than recognizable subjects. He was one of the first artists to develop abstract art.

# STAND-UP CITY

## Make a 3-D version of a Lowry scene!

**1** On a tall piece of cardboard, draw some factory buildings and cut them out along the skyline. Cut window and door shapes from magazines or scrap paper and stick them on.

**2** Make a row of houses in the same way, but not as tall as the factories. To make the buildings stand up, stick cardboard flaps to the back, as shown.

*Fold strips of cardboard and glue them to the back at each side.*

**3** Fold a strip of dark paper back and forth like a concertina. Draw a figure on the top layer with the hands reaching to the sides. Cut it out.

Don't cut here.

*Unfold your chain of people!*

**4** Now you can arrange your scene. Stand the houses in front of the factories and the people in front of them.

You could stick some coloured clothes on the people!

# COMING OUT OF SCHOOL

L. S. Lowry 1927

**Next time you're out, look around you.** Notice people going about their daily lives. Lowry did this all the time! Then he went home and painted what he remembered.

## Dreary day

It looks like a chilly day outside this school. Lowry has used dull greys, browns and blues to show the dreary weather. He was good at capturing moods in this way, only ever using five paint colours. He would daub them on thickly, straight from the tube, blending and scraping with his fingers, a knife, or either end of his brush.

None of the people in this painting have a story. It's just like a glimpse of a moment in time. Lowry painted ordinary, everyday life in the factory towns of northern England. He became famous for his scuttling 'matchstick' figures – someone even wrote a song about them!

## WHO WAS LOWRY?

Laurence Stephen Lowry was born in England in 1887. He spent his adult life working as a rent collector, painting and studying life drawing in his spare time. By the 1950s his work was very popular, even with the Queen! In 1967, *Coming Out of School* was printed on a postage stamp.

# IMAGI-MAP

## Design your own map of a real or imaginary land!

**1** For a watery effect like this, lay out a large piece of cling film and sponge runny blue paint all over it. Press a piece of paper on top then peel it off.

*Experiment with different coloured papers!*

**2** To make the land, scrunch up a piece of thick white paper then open it out. Sprinkle coffee granules over it and rub them in with a damp sponge.

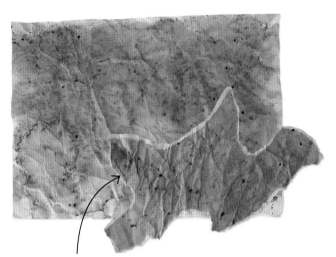

*While the paper is still damp, tear it into ragged shapes.*

*Scrunch up tissue paper for trees.*

**3** Glue the land shapes onto your favourite watery background, then get going with the detail! Cut out paper shapes for animals, buildings, mountains and so on. Stick them all onto your map.

*Make textures by laying tissue paper onto different surfaces and rubbing with a wax crayon.*

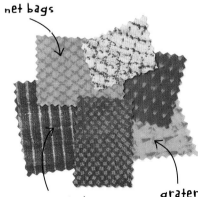
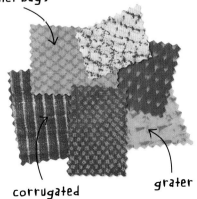

*net bags*

*corrugated card*

*grater*

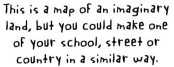

*This is a map of an imaginary land, but you could make one of your school, street or country in a similar way.*

*You could include a colourful compass rose.*

ILLVSTRISS. AC POTENTISS.
REGI FREDERICO II DANIAE,
NORVEGIAE, SLAVORVM, GO-
THORVMQVE REGI, ETC. PRIN
CIPI SVO CLEMENTISSIMO,
ANDREAS VELLEIVS
DESCRIBEB. ET DEDICABAT.

# ISLANDIA

Abraham Ortelius 1592

## Is this a mythical island, with its strange-sounding place names and monsters in the sea?

No, it's an early map of Iceland! Hundreds of years ago, map-makers had to be artists too.

## Masterful mapping

The cartographer who made this map didn't have satellites to help him. It may not be as accurate as maps today, but it is packed with incredible detail. We can see mountains, fjords, rivers, towns and logs from fallen trees. Can you spot the erupting volcano, and icebergs with polar bears perched on top?

Luckily there were notes to explain the weird and wonderful sea creatures. They're a curious mixture of real and legendary beasts. For example, G is an early idea of a seahorse, said to be a threat to fishermen. F, H and L are whales, and K represents sea cows that come onto the land to graze. The sea creature labelled C has a giant head and strong teeth – ideal for making chess pieces!

## WHO WAS ORTELIUS?

Abraham Ortelius was born in what is now Belgium, in 1527. He became famous for producing the first real atlas – the *Theatrum Orbis Terrarum*. His decorative maps were drawn from many sources and printed using engraved copper plates. The atlas was updated, expanded and published 31 times!

# CITY LIGHTS

## Use bright colours against dark ones
**to create a lit-up city scene!**

**1** For the background, use a large piece of black paper or card. Cut a triangle of orange paper to suggest the glare of city lights and glue it on.

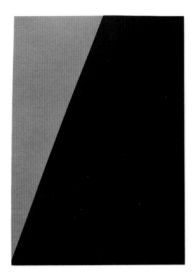

**2** Now cut out some colourful tower blocks and other simple shapes that remind you of a city. Arrange them on the background and glue them down.

You can stick a black building against the orange sky.

**4** To print lines, paint the edge of a piece of cardboard and press it onto the page. For circular shapes, do the same with the rim of a bottle top.

You can print lights with the end of a pencil or a strip of bubble wrap!

**3** To print windows, cover the side or end of a rubber in acrylic paint and press it onto the buildings. Use different surfaces of the rubber to print different shapes.

You could print using pieces cut from a sponge or potato instead.

# NEW YORK
## UNDER GASLIGHT

Stuart Davis 1941

**There's so much to look at in this painting, it's hard to know where to rest your eyes!**
Davis has put together a mass of familiar shapes to create the feel of a busy city.

### City snapshot

Imagine you're rushing down a street – you catch glimpses of shop windows, buildings, signs and other things. That's what Davis shows us. We see a barber's shop and tobacconist, skyscrapers, an overhead canopy, a statue, a flag and a bridge. There are bricks and lettering. Nothing is complete, as if we're just passing quickly by.

Is it day or night in the picture? We can tell from the blazing gas lamp and the moon. The sky is a dusky green, which sits back while the reds, whites and yellows leap towards us. Davis knew that placing bright colours next to duller ones would create the illusion of 3-D space – even though his shapes were completely flat!

## WHO WAS DAVIS?

Stuart Davis was born in the USA in 1892. When he took up art, his teacher encouraged him to use daily life as his subject. He loved painting modern city sights such as electric signs and adverts, and often included words in his scenes. The lively sounds of jazz music also influenced his work!

# OutSide-in

## Make people look twice **with these surreal scenes!**

Magritte's style is called Surrealist, which basically means 'beyond real'. He painted ordinary objects but made us look at them in unusual ways. Because he was so skilled as a painter, he was able to play tricks on the viewer. Many of his pictures look real but impossible at the same time!

**1** On a piece of blue A3 paper, paint some clouds. To do this, dip a cotton wool ball in white paint and dab it on in patches. Cover the page!

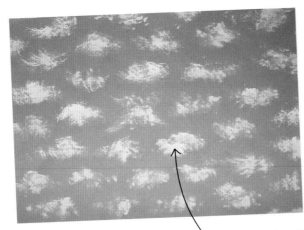

*Dab more lightly in some places for a fluffy effect.*

**2** On a piece of green A4 paper, draw the shape of a tree. Carefully cut it out and keep both pieces.

*Keep the tree shape simple.*

**3** Lay the tree on one side of your cloud page and the outside piece on the other. Glue them down.

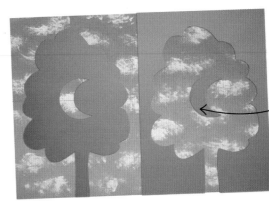

*If you have some spare paper you could stick on a moon shape in the middle.*

**4** What other things can you turn outside-in in the same way? Here are a few ideas!

*Cut out a car and make it fly...*

*...or create a city in the sky!*

*Print bricks by dipping the end of a rubber in brown paint.*

# THE HUMAN CONDITION

René Magritte 1933

**At first this looks like a country scene through a window – then you realize it's a painting of that very scene too!** Magritte loved to make us look twice at his pictures.

## A view – or two?

Can you see the easel and the edge of the canvas in the window? Magritte has covered part of his painting of a view with a painting of a painting that exactly matches it! If that makes you scratch your head, it's meant to. It is a kind of optical illusion – a trick of the eye.

Magritte liked the idea that the tree was both inside the room in the painting and outside in the 'real' landscape. He thought it was similar to the way we see the world. For example, when we look at a chair, the picture we have in our head is the same as the chair, but it isn't the actual chair!

## WHO WAS MAGRITTE?

René Magritte was born in Belgium in 1898. After studying art, he designed wallpaper and posters to earn money while he painted in his spare time. In 1927 he moved to Paris, France, but after a few years he fell out with other Surrealists and went home! Still, he carried on painting in his own Surrealist style.

# ART WORDS AND INFO

**abstract** Not representing an actual object, place or living thing. Abstract art often focuses on simplified shapes, lines, colours, or use of space.

**canvas** A strong type of fabric that artists can paint on.

**cartographer** Someone who makes maps.

**Cubism** (1907–1920s) An art style in which artists, including Gris, made images using simplified shapes and multiple viewpoints.

**easel** A wooden stand that supports an artist's canvas or drawing board.

**engrave** To scratch an image into a hard surface. Prints can be made from designs or lettering engraved on metal sheets.

**foreground** The part of a picture or scene that appears nearest to the viewer.

**geometric shape** A recognizable mathematical shape, such as a triangle.

**horizon** The line, as far away as we can see, where the land or sea seems to meet the sky.

**illusion** Something that seems to be one thing when it's actually another.

**illustration** A picture that explains or decorates a story or other piece of writing.

**impression** An idea or feeling about something.

**landscape** A scene or painting of a scene, usually in the countryside.

**life drawing** Drawing a human figure, often a model in an art class.

**mosaic** A design made up of small pieces of glass, tile or other material, stuck onto a surface.

## COLOUR CONNECTIONS

In art there are three primary colours – **red, yellow** and **blue**. These are colours that can't be mixed from any others. Each primary colour has an opposite, or complementary, which is made by mixing the other two.

If you mix a colour with its complementary, you'll get a shade of brown.

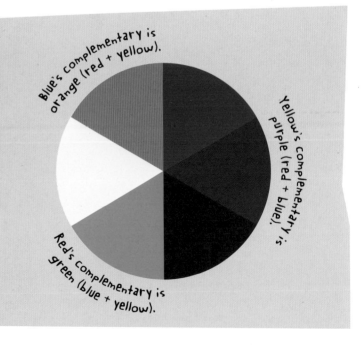

Blue's complementary is orange (red + yellow).

Yellow's complementary is purple (red + blue).

Red's complementary is green (blue + yellow).

**ochre** A brownish yellow colour.

**perspective** The art of showing three-dimensional objects on a flat page, creating the effect of depth or distance.

**print** A way of transferring an image from one surface to another. For example, an artist may carve a design into wood, then cover the raised areas with paint or ink. When this is pressed onto paper, it produces a negative, or reverse, image that can be reproduced many times.

**Prussian blue** A deep, dark blue colour, sometimes known as Berlin blue.

**sketch** A rough drawing or painting, often made to help plan a final artwork.

**smock** A loose type of shirt, worn over clothes to protect them.

**Surrealism** (1924-1940s) An art style that explored the world of dreams, the imagination and the 'non-thinking' mind. Surrealist works often show familiar things in unexpected or impossible ways.

**symbol** A shape or icon that stands for, or represents, something else.

**texture** The feel of a surface, such as rough brick or smooth glass.

**three-dimensional (3-D)** Describes something that has height, width and depth.

**vanishing point** A point on the horizon where parallel lines, such as the sides of a road, appear to meet.

**vibrant** Lively or bright.

# PROJECT CHECKLIST

These are the materials you'll need for each project in this book. The ones in brackets are useful but you can manage without!

**Brush a bedroom** (page 7) thick white paper, pencil, rubber, paper plate or palette, acrylic paints, PVA glue, paintbrushes, (cocktail stick, fork)

**In perspective** (page 9) white paper, pencil, rubber, ruler, coloured pencils or pens, scissors

**Slice a scene** (page 11) thick white paper, pencil, rubber, ruler, acrylic or ready-mix paints, paintbrushes, scissors, glue, large piece of coloured paper

**Castle and moon** (page 13) 2 large sheets of coloured paper (one light, one dark), pencil, rubber, brightly coloured papers, scissors, glue

**Mount Splatter** (page 15) spongy kitchen cloths, scissors, glue, stiff cardboard, acrylic paints, paintbrushes, coloured paper, drinking straw

**Sunset strips** (page 17) thick white paper, pencil, rubber, tissue paper, glue, oil pastels or crayons

**Dotty designs** (page 19) coloured paper, pencil, rubber, acrylic or readymix paints, paintbrush, paper plate

**Rainbow snow** (page 21) coloured pastel paper, pencil, rubber, soft pastels

**Stand-up city** (page 23) cardboard, pencil, scissors, magazines or scrap paper, glue, dark paper

**Imagi-map** (page 25) cling film, blue paint mixed with water, sponge, pale blue papers, thick white paper, coffee granules, glue, scissors, tissue paper, scrap paper, wax crayons, textured surfaces (eg net bags, grater, corrugated card)

**City lights** (page 27) coloured papers, including black and orange, scissors, glue, rubber (or sponge or potato), acrylic paint, paintbrush, paper plate or palette, cardboard, bottle top, pencil (or bubble wrap)

**Outside-in** (page 29) pale blue A3 paper, white acrylic or ready-mix paint, cotton wool ball, A4 green paper, pencil, rubber, scissors, glue, different coloured A4 paper, (brown acrylic paint)

# INDEX